JUN - - 2016

W9-CYD-190

DATE DUE

JUL 1 6 2016	
	PRINTED IN U.S.A.

Yellow Umbrella Books are published by Red Brick Learning
7825 Telegraph Road, Bloomington, Minnesota 55438
http://www.redbricklearning.com

Library of Congress Cataloging-in-Publication Data
Catala, Ellen.
    Who keeps us safe/by Ellen Catala = ¿Quiénes nos protegen?/por Ellen Catala.
    p. cm.
    In English and Spanish.
    Summary: "Simple text and photos present people in the community that keep others safe"—Provided by publisher.
    Includes index.
    ISBN-13: 978-0-7368-6020-8 (hardcover)
    ISBN-10: 0-7368-6020-7 (hardcover)
    1. Police—Juvenile literature. 2. Fire fighters—Juvenile literature. 3. Physicians—Juvenile literature. 4. Teachers—Juvenile literature. 5. Family—Juvenile literature. 6. Bilingual books. I. Title: ¿Quiénes nos protegen? II. Title.
HV7922.C38 2005
363.1—dc22   2005025855

Written by Ellen Catala
Developed by Raindrop Publishing

Editorial Director: Mary Lindeen
Editor: Jennifer VanVoorst
Photo Researcher: Wanda Winch
Adapted Translations: Gloria Ramos
Spanish Language Consultants: Jesús Cervantes, Anita Constantino
Conversion Assistants: Jenny Marks, Laura Manthe

Photo Credits
Cover: Gary Sundermeyer/Capstone Press; Title Page: Richard Hutchings/Corbis; Page 4: Tim Wright/Corbis; Page 6: Table Mesa Productions/Index Stock; Page 8: Grantpix/Index Stock; Page 10: Reed Kaestner/Corbis; Page 12: Frank Siteman/Index Stock; Page 14: PhotoDisc; Page 16: Gary Sundermeyer/Capstone Press

1 2 3 4 5 6 11 10 09 08 07 06

Who Keeps Us Safe?

by Ellen Catala

¿Quiénes nos protegen?

por Ellen Catala

Yellow Umbrella Books

for early readers

Who keeps us safe?

¿Quiénes nos protegen?

Police officers keep us safe.

Los policías nos protegen.

Firefighters keep us safe.

Los bomberos nos protegen.

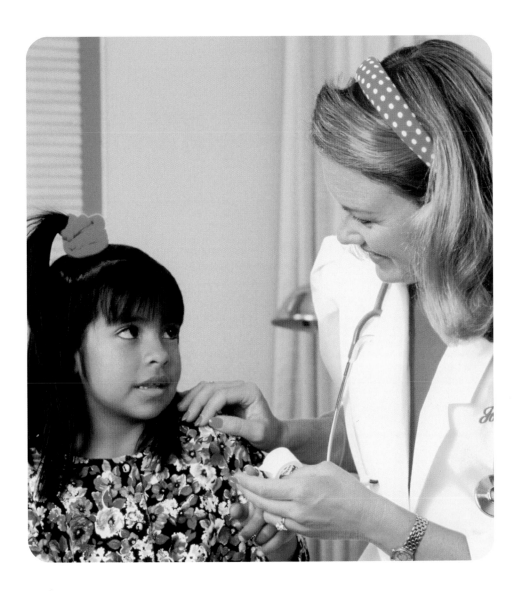

Doctors keep us safe.

Los doctores nos protegen.

Teachers keep us safe.

Los maestros nos protegen.

Families keep us safe.

Nuestras familias nos protegen.

We are safe.

Estamos protegidos.

Index

doctors, 11
families, 15
firefighters, 9

police officers, 7
safe, 5, 7, 9, 11, 13,
15, 17
teachers, 13

Índice

bomberos, 9
doctores, 11
familias, 15

maestros, 13
policías, 7
protegen, 5, 7, 9, 11, 13
15, 17